Understanding Body Language

Understanding Body Language

Geoff Ribbens and Richard Thompson

BARRON'S

All inquiries should be addressed to:
Barron's Educational Series, Inc.
250 Wireless Boulevard
Hauppauge, NY 11788
http://www.barronseduc.com

Library of Congress Catalog Card No. 2001020354

International Standard Book No. 0-7641-1951-6

Library of Congress Cataloging-in-Publication Data
Ribbens, Geoff.
    Understanding body language / Geoff Ribbens, Richard Thompson.
        p. cm.—(Business success series)
    Includes index.
    ISBN 0-7641-1951-6
    1. Nonverbal communication in the workplace.   I. Thompson, Richard,
1946– . II. Title. III. Series.

HF5549.5.N64 R53   2001
650.1′3—dc21   2001020354

PRINTED IN HONG KONG
9 8 7 6 5 4 3 2 1

Contents

◆

Introduction

◆

Body language means more than simply physical posture. Posture and gesture tell you a lot, but so do less obvious mannerisms, such as eye contact, speed and tone of voice, facial expressions, and even nonverbal sounds such as sighs.

We believe that understanding body language in the course of our working lives can help us get ahead, not just because we may look the part, exude confidence, and act assertively, but because we can look beyond what people say to what they really mean.

Though we may not be aware of it, body language is taught to us from the time we are born and we spend years developing skills that enable us to interpret other peoples' intentions, meanings, and motives. Most of us take this learning process for granted, so we tend to forget that much of what happens interpersonally actually takes place at this semiconscious level.

By the end of this book we hope to have convinced you that you can

1. have greater influence.

2. develop effective powers of persuasion.

3. improve interpersonal skills.

4. make more effective presentations.

5. sell more.

6. be more assertive and learn how to control others.

7. reduce negativity and conflict.

8. spot hidden agendas in conversation.

9. enhance your career prospects.

Chapter 1

Body Language

◆

MANAGING WITHOUT WORDS

Would it surprise you to learn that less than 10 percent of the messages we communicate face to face occur through the words we use? If we told you that *tone of voice* accounts for nearly 40 percent and *posture and gesture*, 50 percent, would you believe us? Well, according to the findings of research into body language it is true. You may be asking yourself how that can be possible.

The point is that language is concerned with the expression of thoughts, ideas, and feelings and its function is to enable communication to take place. It doesn't have to be in the form of words, providing that we understand the message and grasp the meaning of what is being conveyed.

Body language does precisely this. By means of nonverbal communication we can convey what we think, how we feel, and what we want. How is this done? Simple. By means of physical posture, gestures, facial expression, tone and strength of voice, and nonverbal sounds. Because we subconsciously use this language in our dealings with others, we tend to take it for granted.

Let us imagine communication without body language. When we write we use commas, periods, exclamation points, and question marks to illustrate to the reader the pauses in our speech and the tone. If we write with no punctuation, it is the same as talking without body language. If we talk without body language the whole meaning and emphasis of what we say is lost.

We recently found this example:

Dear John I want a man who knows what love is all about you are generous kind thoughtful people who are not like you admit to being useless and inferior you have ruined me for other men I yearn for you I have no feelings whatsoever when we're apart I can be forever happy will you let me be yours Gloria

If we now add punctuation, we can make the statement meaningful; however the meaning all depends on where you pause and where you add emphasis.

Dear John,

I want a man who knows what love is all about. You are generous, kind, thoughtful. People who are not like you admit to being useless and inferior. You have ruined me for other men. I yearn for you. I have no feelings whatsoever when we're apart. I can be forever happy. Will you let me be yours?

Gloria

On the other hand if the emphasis is different, we have this message.

Posture congruence

Dear John,

I want a man who knows what love is. All about you are generous, kind, thoughtful people, who are not like you. Admit to being useless and inferior. You have ruined me. For other men, I yearn. For you, I have no feelings whatsoever. When we're apart, I can be forever happy. Will you let me be?

Yours, Gloria

UNCONSCIOUS MIMICRY
As work on body language progressed it was found that people copied each other's behavior without realizing it, sometimes to their advantage, sometimes to their distinct disadvantage.

In the interview situation, for example, it was observed that interviewees responded more positively to questions when interviewers practiced *posture congruence*. This is where body position and hand movements are in harmony between speaker and listener, suggesting that they are getting along with each other.

Mimicry is, in fact, an indirect way of confirming one's common ground with the person you are assessing or trying to convince. In the sales situation, being aware of the customer's body language and reflecting it in your own can be positively advantageous, providing that you don't go too far.

Refinement of ideas such as these throughout the 1970s and 1980s helped to identify a whole range of attitudes and feelings depicted in posture alone. Determination, attentiveness, curiosity, puzzlement, aloofness, indifference, rejection, and self-satisfaction were just some of the more obvious. Even psychiatrists began to realize that they could use their patients' gestures and body postures to evaluate their true feelings and real concerns.

LOW PROFILE, HIGH GAIN

The importance of body language can be seen in the sales situation where sales staff who deliberately avoid the appearance of being the dominant player tend to get the best results.

What this means is that a successful sales pitch depends on staying cool, giving the customer space, using open, friendly gestures, and maintaining—literally—a low profile. Those who appear too defensive or too aloof, on the other hand—particularly on the customer's territory—never get a foot in the door.

What research into body language has proved is that effective management stems from more than just knowledge and words. If these factors were the only important ones, we would probably just send notes to each other. But as most of us know, face-to-face interaction is often the most crucial factor in successfully concluding business, whether it is signing a deal or assessing someone's suitability as a coworker.

> **Note:** You may well be able to gauge an individual's experience and qualifications from a résumé, but you will sum up her potential, honesty, confidence, and abilities in face-to-face contact. This is because observing body language tells you the things that people cannot, will not, or do not wish to say in words. For this reason we still value the face-to-face interview.

INTUITION

There are, however, certain traps in interpreting another person's body language.

What we sometimes put down to *intuition* might well be a combination of things that we have sensed—in other words, feelings that we have at a subconscious level. When it comes to knowing how other people function, intuition could be described as a mixture of unrecognized, nonverbal messages about people and situations, which are constantly being updated by experience.

In a job interview, for example, we often hear people say, "I felt there was something odd about him," or "I should have trusted my intuition." The trouble with relying upon intuition is that we don't always know whether we have sufficient grounds for judging someone, or even whether intuition simply reflects one's personal prejudices.

For this reason, we need to be cautious about interpreting nonverbal communication and just think of it as supplying us with strong clues. After all, posture, gesture, and intonation are subtle and do not, as such, constitute evidence or proof of a way someone thinks or feels. In addition, it is seldom one gesture or posture, but a combination of body signals that convey the clues. It is also important to put the body language in context; for instance, people may rub their hands together because it is cold, not because they are thinking about money.

SEEING IS BELIEVING

The manager who is learning to give presentations may have numerous audiovisual aids at her disposal, but the presentation may flop if she fails to recognize that she is the most important audiovisual aid on the stage. Good presenters need only two things apart from an audience: to be *seen* and to be *heard*.

The more complete the picture of peoples' nonverbal ways of communicating, the more likely it is that you will

◆ understand their motives and feelings.

◆ communicate with them more effectively.

◆ establish a rapport with them more readily.

◆ persuade them without undue opposition.

BODY WORDS

Sometimes, the expressions that people use—yes, the words they actually speak—to describe certain feelings, provide evidence of the close relationship between spoken language and body language. "Down in the mouth," "laid back," "spitting blood," "walking tall," all suggest postures or gestures that represent states of mind.

Because we are rarely aware of these connections, we fail to take full advantage of them. We will be referring to the significance of *body words* as we go along.

The most important visual aid is you

LOOK INTO MY EYES

Eye contact is a fundamental part of getting along with people and gaining their trust. When it is lacking, communication becomes uncomfortable and it is easy to get the wrong impression of what is going on. There's nothing worse than putting on a great show when the parties involved can't be bothered to look at you, or stare with glazed expressions at the wall behind your head.

The gaze, as opposed to the casual glance, tends to convey an interest or intent that has the effect of increasing the other person's awareness of you.

Eye contact also regulates the flow of communication. Briefly holding a look for a few seconds indicates our awareness of what is being said and a readiness to communicate further—somewhat along the lines of "I have finished with that; now I can respond to you on my terms." Waiters in restaurants often use a similar technique of avoiding eye contact with their customers until it suits them to do so, thereby giving the clear message: "I'm too busy to deal with you at the moment." When they finally do look at you directly, you know that you are about to be waited on.

Studies have found that we maintain eye contact with people 40 percent of the time when we are talking to them, yet 75 percent of the time when they are talking to us. As listeners it is important for us to show that we are being attentive to what is being said.

But there is another reason for maintaining eye contact, which has more to do with personal reassurance than respect; it is to determine how sincere the speaker is. What we are doing is summing up how we feel about the speaker by watching her body language and the clues she gives about herself as she performs for us.

I am too busy to deal with you

One of the first things that managers are told when giving presentations is to maintain eye contact with the audience and not to let their eyes wander. If the presenter looks at the screen or flip chart for too long, rapport with the audience is lost and the presentation is considerably weakened.

Communicators who stick to this simple rule are likely to be seen as more persuasive, truthful, sincere, credible, skilled, informed, experienced, honest, and friendly. However unjust it may seem, the confident manager with little knowledge can often outperform the shy but well-informed manager who fails to maintain eye contact with the audience.

The confident presenter maintains eye contact with the people in the audience in a random fashion while keeping them all on their toes. There are always pitfalls, even for the best presenters. We tend to look more at those we like and, if we spot a friendly face or an ally in the audience, we will tend to direct our attention to that person and neglect the rest of the audience—then we will have inadvertently lost most of the listeners.

NLP AND THE MIND'S EYE

In recent years, a body of research, Neurolinguistic Programming, or NLP for short, has suggested that we think in terms of our senses, meaning that the information we draw from the world around us is represented in our minds in the form of pictures, sounds, feelings, smells, and tastes.

Every one of us has preferences for thinking in certain ways, at certain times, and we therefore differ in the ways we perceive and respond to the world around us. Each of the senses have been named:

> - *Visual*—thinking in pictures
> - *Auditory*—thinking in sounds
> - *Kinesthetic*—thinking in feelings
> - *Olfactory*—thinking in terms of smell
> - *Gustatory*—thinking in terms of taste

Depending on which part of the world we come from, cultural differences influence the way in which people think. For example, in the West we are said to think primarily in terms of pictures, sounds, and feelings; those in the East think in terms of smell and taste as well.

The secondary senses, smell and taste, it has been suggested, act as triggers to the primary senses of seeing, hearing, and feeling. For example, the smell of food in an unexpected place might stimulate the mental image of a restaurant that you particularly enjoy. Or the salty taste of sea spray may bring back a nostalgic feeling from a memorable vacation.

Roughly 45 percent of the population are thought to have a primary preference for thinking in terms of feelings (kinesthetic), compared with 35 percent in terms of visual images, and 20 percent in auditory form.

What is interesting about these systems of thinking is that they influence both the choice of words we use in communicating with others, and the body language we exhibit. Eyes are especially indicative of what we are thinking, but it is the direction in which they move that tells us whether we are thinking in terms of pictures, sounds, or feelings.

◆ if we visualize something from past experience our eyes tend to move up and to our left.

◆ if we are trying to construct a picture from words (to imagine something) our eyes move up and to our right.

◆ if we are remembering sounds our eyes move across to our left, although if we are *constructing* sounds they move to our right.

◆ if we are trying to access feelings our eyes move to the right and down.

◆ if we are talking to ourselves our eyes move to the left and down.

◆ if we defocus and stare straight ahead, we are thought to be visualizing, that is, thinking more deeply about the picture in our head.

Access feelings **Talking to ourselves**

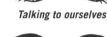

Constructed sounds **Remembered sounds**

Constructed images **Remembered images**

Visualizing

It is possible that looking at the direction of people's eyes could be used by managers in the interview process, but the method is not yet foolproof. For a start, you need to know if the interviewee is left- or right-handed and, given that most people feel uncomfortable when eye contact is maintained for longer than expected, you might make them feel uncomfortable.

BODY THINKING

The point about all of this is that if thinking processes are reflected in the way we use our eyes, they probably manifest themselves in other forms of body language as well. "As the body and mind are inseparable," it has been written, "how we think always shows somewhere, if you know where to look. In particular, it shows in breathing patterns, skin color, and posture."

And if the mind–body link is true, managers, for example, could benefit from knowing how eye movements convey different kinds of thought processes, thereby enhancing their interpersonal skills.

But what evidence is there to back up such a claim? Here are some examples.

Thinking in visual images

When people do this they tend to speak more quickly and at a higher pitch. In addition, their breathing may be high in the chest and more shallow. There is often an increase in muscle tension, particularly in the shoulders, the head will be up, and the face will often appear paler than normal.

Thinking in sounds

In this case, people tend to breathe evenly over the whole chest area. Small rhythmic movements of the body are discernible and voice tonality is clear, expressive, and resonant. The head is well balanced on the shoulders, or held slightly at an angle as if listening to something.

Talking to oneself

When people do this they often lean their heads to one side, resting it on their hand or fist. This is known as the "telephone position," as they seem to be talking on an invisible telephone. They may actually repeat out loud what they have just "heard," with the result that you can see their lips move.

Thinking about feelings

This is characterized by deep breathing low in the stomach area. The voice has a deeper tonality to it and the person will typically speak slowly, using long pauses. The body language implicit in Rodin's famous sculpture of *The Thinker* could be said to suggest kinesthetic thinking.

It has also been observed that when we are involved in different kinds of thinking processes we often gesture toward the sense organ related to it. For example, some people gesture in the direction of their ears while listening to sound cues; others may point to their eyes when visualizing. If we feel things particularly strongly, we sometimes gesture toward the abdomen.

Although these examples indicate how people think in relation to how they act, they do not necessarily tell us what they are thinking. For counselors and job interviewers, who must interpret what they hear, such techniques could nevertheless provide valuable clues.

GETTING IT TOGETHER

If people think in terms of pictures, sounds, and feelings, then how do we know if two people are thinking along the same lines? For example, if we are talking together in coaching, training, sales, counseling, or other similar situations, and we are thinking in different modes, isn't it going to be difficult to establish a meaningful rapport?

What is likely to occur is that a conversation between a person thinking *visually* and a person thinking in *feelings* could turn out to be a frustrating experience for both parties. The visual thinker will probably be tapping a foot impatiently, while the feeling thinker literally won't see why the other has to go so quickly. A positive result is likely to depend on who first adapts to the other's way of thinking.

So what does all this tell us about the relationship between body language and thought processes? Well, one thing is for sure: If you want to establish a rapport with someone, being on the same wavelength is a good start. In the past, this might simply have meant responding as well as possible to how you believe the other person will react. Now, with the advantage of knowing that we think in different modes, we can perhaps fine-tune our response by using words similar to those of the person we are talking to.

BODY TALK

Visual thinkers are more likely to use visual expressions such as "I *see* what you mean," "Can we get that in *focus*," "It seems *hazy* to me," whereas *auditory thinkers* would say such things as "That *sounds* strange to me," "I *hear* what you are saying," and so forth.

Kinesthetic thinkers, on the other hand, would say such things as "It doesn't *feel* right to me," "My *gut* reaction is to say No," or "I can't *grasp* that idea." By reflecting back the same words, the sensitive manager can maintain rapport in such areas as selling, counseling, interviewing, or evaluating. Managers noted for their social skills will often be on the same wavelength as others because they consciously or subconsciously adopt the same speech patterns and words.

SUMMARY

So, if you find yourself feeding back a few of the words that the other person is using because you feel that you are on common ground, it is probably due to your increasing awareness of them. You are becoming more socially and emotionally intelligent.

Chapter 2

Actions Speak Louder Than Words

POSTURE AND GESTURE

To a very large extent, we physically dance to the tune of our thoughts, conveying meaning and feeling through our actions. Gesticulations, head movements, and body posture all add emphasis to what we are saying, investing our words with meaning, and adding to the impression we create.

Sometimes, thoughts and feelings that we try to hide behind our words creep out in our posture and gestures. Not surprisingly, as listeners, we rely heavily on what someone's body language tells us before we make up our minds about them.

Many types of posture and a variety of gestures—such as the raising of eyebrows when we meet—are common to people of all cultures, while others, especially certain hand gestures, are culturally specific and you have to be a little careful how you use them in different countries.

For example, in the United States, when the thumb and forefinger make a circle, this means "OK," while in Brazil it represents an insult similar to the American raised middle finger. In Japan, however, it means "money," and in France "zero."

In Europe, scratching your head can mean you are puzzled about something, whereas in Japan it is often an indication of anger.

UK and USA = O.K.

JAPAN = MONEY

BRAZIL = INSULT

FRANCE = ZERO

> We not only make assumptions about people's moods and feelings from postures and gestures, but also tend to view those who exhibit a greater variety of body language in a more positive light. Studies have found that people who communicate nonverbally through active movement tend to be rated as *warm*, more *casual*, *agreeable*, and *energetic*, while those who remain still are seen as *logical*, *cold*, and *analytic*.

POSTURE

Anger, excitement, shyness, rejection
You can often tell a person's attitude from his body language. Anger tends to be conveyed by leaning forward, sometimes with fists clenched and a tight facial expression. Excitement is often exhibited in an open body position, arms raised up, palms up, with mouth and eyes wide open. Shyness is usually conveyed by looking down, making little eye contact, and leaning to one side, while rejection tends to be exhibited by turning the face and body away.

Intimidation

How a person stands can indicate not only how he feels, but also how he views a situation—in other words, his attitude toward someone or something. A very upright stance can appear threatening, particularly when your territory, such as your office, is invaded by someone marching in and standing very close to you.

Senior managers who act in this way toward their subordinates are, not surprisingly, seen as intimidating. Therefore, to maintain rapport with others, it is advisable, particularly if you are tall, to reduce your height—lean on something; stoop slightly.

People of high status often stand with their hands on their hips and with elbows turned out. This is a posture of superiority and exemplifies *dominance*. Sitting with legs in the four-cross position—with the ankle of one leg resting on the knee of the other—with elbows

| Depressed | Rejecting | Excited |
| Defensive | Thoughtful | Confident |

Posture of superiority

outstretched and hands clasped behind the neck, head, or back similarly suggest superiority. It is not uncommon to see two equal-status male executives in discussion subconsciously adopting similar postures in order to maintain their respective positions of authority.

Defensiveness

When you see someone sitting in a meeting with his arms crossed, what do you make of it? True, this often happens when chairs have no armrests, but it could mean that the person concerned is being *defensive*. Any hunching of the back or clenching of the fists—even if the individual is unaware that this is happening—can be interpreted as *aggressive-defensive*, or even *hostile*.

Posture not only reflects feelings, but also *intentions*.

Interest—indifference

People subconsciously indicate positive interest in others by propping their heads up on a hand with the index finger pointing up over the cheek. Critical appraisal is similarly indicated by an attentive gaze with the chin resting on a thumb and the fingers touching or covering the mouth. These are quite commonly observed in meetings among buyers or senior executives when they are evaluating other peoples' comments.

Leaning forward in your chair suggests that you are reacting positively to what you are hearing and that you may be about to act on a particular suggestion. On the other hand, leaning backwards tends to indicate indifference, or a lack of interest.

Inappropriate posture
Inappropriate body language can be insulting or annoying. Some people deliberately use it for this purpose. Coming across as too forceful or too relaxed can be offensive. For example, sitting slumped in a chair with your head down when someone is talking

Seated readiness posture

to you displays indifference toward the speaker. Similarly, sitting with one leg over the arm of a chair suggests casual indifference.

As a rule of thumb we would advise against the use of overly casual body language, particularly in situations in which you are dealing with valued clients or subordinates.

Cultural differences can sometimes lead to erroneous conclusions about posture. American men, for example, often sit with their legs in the four-cross pattern. European men will often just cross one leg over the other, which is perceived in the United States as an effeminate posture.

Male body language in the company of women during meetings sometimes produces the unexpected. One study found that when a woman was present in a standing group, those men who were attracted to her pointed their feet in her direction—even when they were talking to their male colleagues.

Male pair and female pair exhibiting posture congruence

Copycat behavior

We have already referred to posture congruence in which people imitate or mirror each other's posture, often without realizing it. *Interactional synchronizing* occurs when people simultaneously move at the same time in the same way, such as picking up coffee cups or starting to speak at exactly the same moment; this often occurs when people are getting along well together. It is almost as if we are echoing each other; in fact, we are responding subliminally to our partners' subtle cues.

Opening up

It takes time for people to feel comfortable with a superior and, as many body language experts will testify, if you can get an individual to open up physically, the chances are that he will open up emotionally as well. Crossed arms, legs, or ankles, self-hugging, chin down, and a slumped appearance are all telltale signs that something is wrong.

Discussing the subject of bullying at work, one expert pointed out that when someone is bullied, he may feel depressed, making him slump down and lean forward. If the person being bullied stands up straight instead, he won't feel as depressed. Conversely, when we feel angry we tense up, clench our fists, and tighten our jaw, so that being persuaded to loosen up can have the opposite effect of what is intended and we won't feel as angry.

What this means is that you need to find a way to gently break the ice. One way is to offer tea or coffee. Though this may sound simplistic, it is nevertheless the case that people find it difficult to raise a cup to their mouths with their legs crossed, and totally impossible with their arms crossed. Thus, by such a simple procedure, you enable your closed individual to literally open up.

GESTURE

If body posture subconsciously reflects feelings, mood, and thought, gestures consciously convey emotion and meaning. This doesn't mean you know exactly what you are doing all of the time; rather, it means that there is a greater degree of conscious awareness about your actions than in the case of body posture.

We generally gesture with our hands, arms, head, and shoulders, in order to add emphasis to what we are saying.

Active interest, listening, and concern

A common gesture of television interviewers and their guests is the head cock, where the head is tilted to one side. This indicates active listening, interest, and concern. Nodding the head slowly while listening indicates "I hear you and understand," whereas more rapid nods mean "I hear you and agree with you."

A word of warning to interviewers—the head nod that one generally regards as meaning Yes, often means No in Bulgaria, parts of Greece, Yugoslavia, Turkey, Iran, and Bengal!

Confidence, aloofness, submission, aggression

Generally speaking, when the head is held up and the face points in an upward direction, this indicates confidence and, in some cases, aloofness, or even a patronizing attitude toward others. Lowering the head and avoiding eye contact is more suggestive of submissive behavior. When someone thrusts his head and chin forward, he may be signaling alarm or aggressiveness, particularly if the eyes are wide open at the same time.

Don't care, waste of time

A common gesture is the shrug where both shoulders are raised and often accompanied by the palms-up hand gesture. These usually indicate that the person concerned doesn't care, doesn't know, or thinks whatever is happening is a waste of time.

Disagreement

Certain gestures that we use can appear at odds with what we are saying. Take the case in which a listener tells the speaker that he is in agreement, yet his head appears to move slightly from side to side rather than up or down thus signaling *dis*agreement. In such cases it may be that the listener simply cannot be bothered to argue; in other words, his real feelings are indicated by the head shake.

While some individuals will show disagreement by shaking their heads, others do so less obviously by "picking lint"—picking imaginary pieces of fluff off their clothes. Whether consciously intended or not, this conveys the message "I disagree with you, but I can't be bothered to argue about it."

HAND GESTURES

The handshake—strength or weakness?
In different countries and cultures, similar gestures have different meanings and can easily give rise to misunderstandings. For example, one of the most commonly used gestures in corporate life is the handshake.

Whereas in the United States and western Europe a firm handshake is associated with positiveness, conviction, strength, openness, and honesty, in the Indian subcontinent a limp handshake is the norm, representing a different perception of what is positive.

Hand cupping—domination and control
Hand gestures can be used to express negative as well as positive feelings, such as annoyance, aggression, and insults. People who choose to shake hands by placing one hand over (rather than to the side of) the other person's hand want to assert their dominance.

Fist and finger insults
Fist waving and the single finger pointing upwards are both insults. In fact, pointing is generally regarded as rude or aggressive and should be avoided when possible in the context of business interaction. It is more socially acceptable to direct an upraised palm than to point at someone in a meeting.

Though in much of Europe tapping the forefinger on the side of the head is widely recognized as signifying "You're crazy," the Dutch tap the center of the forehead, while the French make a circular motion at the side of the head.

The hand shrug—mock honesty
In conversation a palms-up gesture tends to indicate uncertainty, though with a degree of honesty. But it can also be used to deceive.

The hand shrug, as it is known, is one of those mock honesty gestures that appears to enlist our sympathy by giving the impression that the other person has our best interests at heart despite being unsure of the outcome.

Patting, tapping, thumping, fiddling
When someone places his hands palms down in a patting fashion, along with raised eyebrows, he is probably indicating satisfaction with, or certainty about the facts placed before him. If this patting continues it most likely means "I have heard what you have to say so please calm down." Tapping one's fingers on a desk is a sign of impatience, while banging or thumping clearly indicates annoyance and aggression. Fiddling with pencils during meetings suggests boredom or irritation.

"Trust me—I'm in marketing."

Steepling

Steepling—confidence, certainty

A common gesture often seen in corporate situations is steepling, where both hands are close together with fingertips touching, but with palms a short distance apart—quite literally in the shape of a church steeple.

Often unconsciously performed, this action has been interpreted as indicating a sense of confidence, or as suggesting that the individual concerned has come to a decision. Clearly this has significance in the sales situation.

Palm rocking—"maybe"

Another hand gesture often noticed among younger executives is palm rocking with fingers spread out. Called the "so-so," it involves placing the palm face down and rocking it from side to side. This is taken to mean something similar to the verbal "-ish," meaning "maybe," "possibly," "OK."

Thumbs up

You would think that the ubiquitous thumbs-up gesture would be commonly understood as meaning "OK," "everything's fine," and so forth, but it isn't. In Australia, if made with a jerk, it means "Up yours!" and in Nigeria it is also regarded as rude. In Germany, when you order drinks, it means "One, please."

DECEPTION GESTURES

Rubbing, scratching, touching

There are gestures of which we are hardly aware, such as touching our noses when we are not telling the truth, or when we believe someone is trying to deceive us.

Scratching one's neck with the index finger about five times below the ear, while the neck is turned slightly to one side, indicates doubt and uncertainty. This gesture is common among car mechanics

Keep it a secret.

who also tend to suck in air between the teeth when asked how long it will take and how much it will cost to repair your car!

Sometimes when people are not telling the truth they rub their eye while looking down as if they are distracted by a piece of grit, when in fact, this gesture is designed to distract the attention of the listener.

When you see someone tap the side of his nose with his forefinger, this can indicate a desire for confidentiality or secrecy, although the gesture differs in meaning between cultures.

In Britain and Sardinia, the nose tap conveys complicity, confidentiality, or secrecy, while in Italy it means "Be alert." In Britain, Holland, and Austria, if the tap is to the front of the nose, it means "Mind your own business."

In some situations, placing a hand over the nose suggests both fear and disbelief, as if one does not wish to comprehend or accept what is going on.

SUMMARY

The body language of posture and gesture really can be quite revealing. One thing's for sure, you'll never take it for granted again.

Chapter 3

Power and Influence

THE ROAD TO SUCCESS

Success has as much to do with being perceived as doing your job well as actually doing it well. It's a simple—although perhaps not always welcome—fact of life that conveying the right impression can make up for deficiencies in knowledge and skills. Many talented people fail to be promoted because they make the mistake of thinking that success is judged on the basis of *what* they do well, rather than the *impression* they create in doing it.

As we have already seen in Chapter 2, understanding body language can make executives more effective. Effective leaders not only spend time on the job at hand, but also on the needs of the individuals who make up the team. Sensitivity to such needs increases effectiveness and influence—advantages achieved as a result of enhanced interpersonal skills.

By not understanding the subtleties of body language you are at a disadvantage in the communication process. A lack of awareness of the nonverbal signals that people give automatically limits your insight into their behavior and intentions.

THE BODY LANGUAGE OF POWER

Many of the words we use to describe interaction with authority figures reflect characteristics of the body language of power. For example, an influential member of a staff may be said to be "close to the boss," when the boss allows that person to occupy her physical space. When we say, "She has the boss's ear" (or eye for that matter), we mean she is close enough to the boss to say things in private. "He's the boss's right-hand man" not only signifies personal influence, but a close liaison with the person in authority.

Some individuals try to influence their superiors by adopting a subservient approach. This can result in derogatory comments about apple polishing or worse, characteristics of behavior that Dickens epitomized in the character of the obsequious Uriah Heep in *David Copperfield*. The clear indication is that people who lower themselves physically diminish the respect accorded to them. Pushy people, on the other hand, are often those who try to get around the boss, thereby gaining access to authority at the expense of others.

When we describe someone as *straightforward*, we mean open and honest, while *warped* or *twisted* signifies the opposite. Similarly, someone who is *upright* is to be trusted, and the person who *walks tall* feels confident and proud. Individuals who see others as inferior look *down* on them or *down* their noses at them. Lifting the head slightly while doing this is an expression of contempt. All these terms refer to the posture associated with power or the lack of it.

Keeping someone at arm's length or *not crowding her space* literally means not getting too close to her. We often take these words and phrases for granted without realizing that they are descriptions of body language cues that we witness all the time.

POWERBROKING

People get where they are because they adopt different strategies for increasing their authority over others. Among these are five sources of power:

1. *Position*—who they are

2. *Coercive*—how tough they are

3. *Reward*—how supportive they are

4. *Expertise*—how informed they are

5. *Charisma*—how unique they are

POSITION POWER

JOHN TITLE

My power in this company comes from people knowing who I am. I'm a senior supervisor and this means that the staff should respect my authority. We should look up to our superiors; after all, that's what super (= above) + visor (= look) means. Others look up to me. I have access to the boss because of my position in the company.

Powerbrokers who rely upon who they are in the company are not difficult to spot. They adopt the postures, gestures, and unspoken cues associated with hierarchical authority. The most casual of observers will generally be able to pick out the boss in a group by the respective body language of superior and subordinate. Typically, the boss will adopt a posture of superiority or will look down on others.

The significant thing about position power is that it is the minimum form of authority that a manager has. People still tend to obey managers out of respect for the title, even if the individual fails in all other aspects of the job.

Power and *status symbols*, such as your own office, car, uniform, or where you sit in a restaurant, can be used to advantage. Common power gestures include hands on hips with elbows out, holding the lapel with thumbs up, hands in pockets with thumbs out, or head up looking down the nose.

An executive we came across used to make people wait outside her door for longer than might be expected after they had knocked, and then shout "Come in!" in an irritated tone. This had the effect of making the employee feel uncomfortable about entering the executive's territory. The executive would continue writing, thus giving the impression that she was not to be disturbed. After a further period, she would look up slowly while replacing her pen cap and, with a degree of impatience, tell the unfortunate individual to go back and close the door. Through her body language and tone of voice she reminded her subordinates of their relative positions.

In recent years, cyclical changes in general economic conditions have brought about a fundamental reappraisal of organizational structures and patterns of employment, with the result that attitudes to hierarchical authority have altered. *Horizontal* (expertise) rather than *vertical* (position) lines of authority make for greater cooperation and encourage upward mobility.

The acceptance of a more egalitarian approach to employment and management has been shown to increase personal commitment to employers and to boost production. By reducing status barriers, communication is increased and flexibility in working practices is encouraged.

Managers these days are expected to facilitate not merely administer. In the future, the term *manager* may well disappear, as the terms *foreman* and *supervisor* are slowly disappearing. The decline of these terms means the decline of position power and the rise of reward power and expert power.

COERCIVE POWER

PHIL HARDMAN

You have to be tough and decisive to manage. If managers fail to confront or to discipline lazy employees, they won't be respected by the rest of the workforce.

Threats enhance respect for a manager. How many times have you heard someone say, "He's fair, but I wouldn't get *on the wrong side* of him if I were you."

The strong manager doesn't hem and haw about things, or ask if everything's OK with you. Just hold your gaze, stand straight, and don't move around, because that suggests you are wavering.

The body language of coercion is not difficult to recognize, its most common expression being aggression, which is characterized by overt postures and gestures that are designed to threaten, such as

◆ the upright stance, standing with hands on hips, or sitting in a dominant position.

◆ an expressionless or angry look.

◆ the invasion of another's space.

◆ shouting.

◆ finger pointing.

- ◆ staring at a subordinate.

- ◆ strutting down corridors in a way that conveys the impression that no one will get in your way.

- ◆ turning away when someone else is talking.

- ◆ peppering conversation with snorts of derision, annoyance, or disgust.

- ◆ frowning, or jutting the chin out.

- ◆ clenching the fist.

However, coercive power can also be self-defeating. Threats of a negative review or, demotion and nonverbal intimidation—invasion of personal space, the upright stance, staring—can mean that the manager will not have a loyal and motivated workforce and will have to bear the extra cost of high staff turnover.

Finger pointing

To resort to coercive methods when the situation genuinely requires it, such as firing someone for gross misconduct, may be acceptable, although you need to be aware of your motives. Be sure that coercion is not being used to boost your own ego. In the long run, the latent threat of coercive action tends to prove more effective.

REWARD POWER

JILL MERIT

Staff in my company obey their superiors because they know that they will ultimately be rewarded in some way. The culture promotes this. Perhaps we're different, but we know how to keep our employees happy. It's not bribery; it's sympathetic management.

We are not in a position to increase salaries at the drop of a hat, but we can reward people with more interesting work, a glowing appraisal, and more responsibility, giving them a sense of achievement and empowering them.

Unlike monetary rewards, psychological encouragement is conveyed nonverbally through tone of voice and gestures, and needs to be sincere if it is to have the desired effect of motivating and boosting morale. There are many ways in which managers can reward employees in this way. For example:

◆ the longer-than-average handshake or the handclasp to emphasize a job well done.

◆ a light touch or pat on the back to express praise or congratulations; touching someone on the shoulder as she leaves is a subtle way of rewarding good work and showing rapport.

◆ the smile and a slightly longer look to denote thanks.

◆ a slight nod of the head to suggest agreement or recognition.

We often use body language expressions with reference to rewarding people without necessarily realizing the connection between the emotion and the physical action: "I was touched," "I had to hand it to her," "It was only a small gesture," "He deserves a pat on the back for that."

EXPERT POWER

DR. GRAHAM SURE

Being recognized as experts in our field increases our influence and control. How else do you think we get our research funding? This is where the advantages of body language come in. If I appear hesitant, look puzzled, fail to make adequate eye contact, speak without self-assurance, come across as nonassertive and lacking in confidence, this makes people question my competence, because I appear unsure.

Nonexpert	Expert
I *hope* that you will enjoy this presentation.	I *know* that you will appreciate what I have to say.
I *think* that is most *probably* the answer.	Under these circumstances this is what we *should* do.

The emphasis placed on these words is all-important.

Assertive body language conveys confidence and suggests expertise. The way you stand, or the way in which you pay attention to others gives an impression of certainty, self-assurance, and a sense that you feel good about yourself. Simple things such as looking at the other person and steepling, where the finger tips are touching but the palms are apart (see page 29), show that you are interested in what you are being told. This type of relaxed body language exudes confidence. Turning the hands palms down and appearing to press downward while talking to others also has the effect of making them listen and look up to you.

Research in Neurolinguistic Programming has shown that we condition ourselves to succeed or fail by our thought processes. By self-conditioning—maintaining an internal dialogue that reinforces personal successes—we can make ourselves feel more confident, thereby making us more influential. Confident words should be used with confident posture and gestures:

◆ Use positive-sounding words and emphasize your certainty at all times.

◆ When talking, hold your palms down to express certainty.

◆ When sitting, use the steeple position of the hands (palms apart, fingertips touching) to show that you are in touch with what is going on.

◆ Stand upright, maintain an open stance, and smile.

◆ Walk with an upright posture as if you know where you are going.

◆ Keep your head up, but don't look down your nose.

◆ Precondition yourself to succeed. Above all, have faith in yourself and your abilities.

CHARISMA

A FAN

When he walked into the room I was mesmerized. I couldn't take my eyes off him. I don't know what it was. He had a sort of aura, a self-assurance without arrogance—a presence.

He didn't even have to speak. There were people buzzing around him like flies and yet he seemed totally unconcerned. I was the one feeling nervous.

How lucky to be like that. Some people just have that indefinable quality, don't they? That *je ne sais quoi.*

Social psychologists have long tried to establish the link between *leadership* and *charisma* and have found that charisma itself resides in the minds of the followers, not in the traits of the leader.

This means that it is our perceptions of a colleague's or competitor's abilities that invest that individual with charismatic power rather than the abilities themselves. So, we should be seeking evidence of charismatic body language in the audience—among the believers.

When a charismatic person enters a room, others move away to give her space. Sometimes it is simply the hush that descends on the gathering that tells you someone is highly regarded. Charismatic people often seem tall to the observer because people tend to bow slightly—literally lowering their height in front of their leader.

Charismatic people are also said to radiate power, energy, and love, and yet this radiation comes from the audience in response to the admired person.

Charismatic authority, therefore, is a social property—invested in the highly regarded or venerated people by others, and maintained by that person through constant reinforcement of those characteristics most admired.

Sometimes we refer to these special people as being *head and shoulders above the rest*. These are the ones who are *up front, firm, rock steady*, even *having us in the palms of their hands*. We respect them for their leadership, aware that there is something about their presence that denotes authority.

MORE ON ASSERTIVENESS

What is assertiveness and its value in terms of body language?

There are four styles of behavior that all of us characterize from time to time: *aggressive*, *submissive*, *assertive*, and *manipulative*. Some people are disproportionately more aggressive or submissive than others and, as a result, tend to be thought of in these terms.

Assertiveness basically means declaring your position in a firm, open, and reasonable manner. The professional manager who is firm, but fair generally feels more confident about handling difficult situations, improves business outcomes, gets the best out of other people, and actually reduces conflict with and between them. Often, this means that she is able to manage without words, to make others aware of her views and feelings via the subtle nuances of body language.

There is little doubt that managerial effectiveness can be enhanced by a greater understanding of body language. Successful managers are those who feel comfortable about being assertive and display their expertise and leadership qualities through self-assured and confident behavior.

THE BODY LANGUAGE OF POWER

Aggressive	
Description	*Body language*
Angry, sarcastic, being a bad listener, putting people down, blaming others, shouting, raising one's voice, overly critical.	Clenched fists, confrontational pose, tense body posture, hands on hips, head tilted, finger pointing, prolonged eye contact, narrowing eyes, looking down on others.
Manipulative	
Description	*Body language*
Patronizing, crafty, calculating, insincere, two-faced, a "user," lacking trust, overly friendly, making ends justify means, contrived, etc.	Exaggerated gestures (such as open palms to indicate deliberate sincerity), overly laid back posture, patronizing touching, exaggerated eye contact, sugary voice tone, patting.

Continued

Submissive

Description
Apologetic, self-deprecating, resentful, low self-esteem, retreating, too ready to please.

Body language
Fidgety, covering mouth and eyes, slumped posture, nervous disposition, fiddling, poor eye contact, quiet, faltering voice, pleading smile, tendency toward obsequiousness.

Assertive

Description
Sincere, open, honest, respectful, sympathetic, firm but fair, offering constructive criticism, good listener, offering praise where it is due, treating people as equals.

Body language
Upright, relaxed posture, face-to-face eye contact, calm and open gestures, relaxed facial expression, maintaining reasonable distance from subject (not too close for comfort), resonant speech, unambiguous hand signals.

Chapter 4

Performance Art

PRESENTATION SKILLS

> *Brilliance without the capability to communicate is worth little in any enterprise.*   Thomas Leech, 1982.

Every presentation you make is essentially a *performance*, in which the hearts and minds of the audience are there to be won over. As we noted earlier, as much as 90 percent of what we communicate is transmitted nonverbally, which means that a large part of our performance relies upon *presence*, as opposed to words, technical support, or gimmickry. No matter how many visual aids you have at your disposal, nothing is ultimately as visually persuasive as you.

It is perhaps no accident that highly successful presenters are described as having their audiences "in the palm of their hands," when you consider that the up-turned palm has traditionally been associated with gestures of honesty, openness, and sincerity.

Before beginning a presentation, make sure you know what you are trying to do. For example, do you aim to inform, instruct, persuade, entertain, justify, or sell? The objective must be clear to you, but not necessarily clear to the audience.

Salespeople know that by overstating their intention to sell, they increase the resistance on the part of their clients to buy. But by subtle use of body language and tone of voice you can convince an audience that you are simply there to inform.

RULES OF ENGAGEMENT

Maintain eye contact with the audience
Members of your audience need to believe that you are talking to each of them as individuals. They need to feel that your random glance during a sweep of the room is at them in particular, and that you are only looking at everyone else out of politeness.

Remember, presenters who maintain regular eye contact with the audience are more likely to be perceived as being persuasive, sincere, credible, honest, experienced, and friendly.

Be aware of hand gestures and tone of voice
If eye contact is important in gaining the attention of your audience, how you *act* and *sound* is just as important in maintaining it.

The facts are as follows

Your hands should conduct your presentation as if it were the slow movement of a symphony, fingers and palms modulating with your words.

When presenting facts, it helps to hold the hands out and the palms down as this indicates assurance and certainty. Conversely, if you hold your palms up when delivering facts, you may be perceived as uncertain and your message as confusing.

Speak slowly, adding emphasis where appropriate by varying the tone and resonance of your voice. Speaking more quickly to make a particular point is fine, providing that your audience can hear and understand you. Very often, presenters speed up when they start to feel confident about the presentation and lose sections of the audience as a result.

Repeat key phrases to reinforce your message

One way of adding emphasis in a presentation is to repeat key phrases using an assertive tone of voice. The actual words themselves need not always be repeated providing that the *meaning* remains the same. In selling, for example, one might say, "There are four main selling points to this product. The four points are . . . Let us look at one in detail and then go through the other three."

Use visual aids to structure your presentation

Maintaining eye contact with the audience while making use of prompting techniques and facilities is not always easy. One method is to use note cards, which are held in the palm of the hand and require you to take your eyes off the audience only momentarily. These cards should contain only key words—reminders of what you wish to say—and nothing else.

Another, and perhaps better, way is to use words on the screen or flip chart as *key word prompts* and as a means of structuring your presentation. Structuring can also be done by means of a flip chart, which leads you to issues and ideas that indicate your intention to move from one area to the next. Typical expressions for use in such situations might be, "Moving on now to item three," or "I would now like to examine the outcome."

Whatever you do, do not allow a visual aid to distract you from those you are addressing. The moment you start to pay less attention to the audience, the audience starts to pay less attention to you.

The audience will pay less attention to you if you turn your back.

BE ANIMATED BUT STAY CALM AND LOOK PROFESSIONAL

There are a number of common distractions that reduce audience attention. For example, do not

◆ march from one side of the stage to the other.

◆ fiddle with pointers, pens, and other items.

◆ seek confirmation with such phrases as "Is that okay?" "Do you see?" or "You know what I mean?"

◆ stand with your hands in your pockets; the posture gives the impression that you are overconfident, but more important, if your hands are in your pockets you cannot use them to gesture and emphasize your words.

HOLD AUDIENCE ATTENTION BY SOUNDING ENTHUSIASTIC

It is generally accepted that for all presentations there is an *attention curve*. Audience attention will be high at the beginning, low in the middle, and higher at the end. If your presentation is long— more than 30 minutes—you should try to hold audience attention by sounding more enthusiastic as you go along. Enthusiasm is powerfully expressed through body language and can be infectious.

HOLD THE AUDIENCE'S ATTENTION BY HAVING A NATURAL BREAK

Another way of holding the audience's attention is to have a natural break in the middle of your presentation, for example, by passing around items, samples, and literature. But if you are going to do this, keep the materials hidden from view in the beginning, otherwise, they will distract attention from you.

TAKE NOTE OF NEGATIVE BODY LANGUAGE

The more skilled you become in recognizing the meanings implicit in gesture and posture, the more control you will have over your audience. Certain gestures and postures tell you a lot about people's attitude toward you and their receptiveness to what you are saying.

◆ Leaning the chin on a hand with the index finger on the cheek indicates critical appraisal or critical evaluation.

◆ The steepling gesture indicates that someone has made up his mind, either for or against you.

◆ Sitting with arms and ankles crossed indicates that someone may feel defensive.

◆ Picking lint from clothes indicates that someone disagrees but does not want to argue with you.

If you are aware of these things happening, try to draw the people concerned into the dialogue. One way to do this is to invite comments from the audience by directing your line of sight to the person who seems to not agree with what you are saying. For example, "I'm sure I haven't convinced all of you, so perhaps, someone can tell me—what sort of concerns do you think people

Critical appraisal

Picking at clothing: silent disagreement

might have about this?" By keeping your question impersonal you are more likely to get him to drop his defenses and air his views.

AVOID BEING DISTRACTED BY MEMBERS OF THE AUDIENCE

Because body language is a two-way process, presenters, whether they are aware of it or not, respond to cues and signals given by members of the audience. There are some common pitfalls associated with this.

1. The "friendly" individual who is clearly paying attention and who nods and occasionally smiles in response to the presenter's points. The presenter may unwittingly direct his attention to that person, thus breaking the visual link with the rest of the audience.

2. The one-to-one conversation where the presenter gets caught up in a question-and-answer situation with a single member of the audience. All too often this makes other members of the audience feel excluded.

ATTEMPT TO ENCOURAGE CONVERGENCE OF OPINIONS

In any audience there are bound to be differences of opinion and the astute presenter can often identify sets or subgroups of people who appear to share similar opinions. This is particularly important in negotiations or meetings in which the goal is to achieve a consensus.

As we have already observed, when people establish a rapport they often mirror each other's gestures and postures—posture congruence. For example, you might be in a meeting in which people from the personnel department appear to be sharing the same body posture. The engineers on the other side of the table, however, are sitting with necks bowed and arms folded. What do you make of this? Do you conclude that the engineers are being defensive and their

Personnel   *Engineering*

body language indicates that a lot of work still needs to be done before they are won over? If so, what is your strategy for dealing with the situation?

What you need to do is encourage participation.

◆ Mention their names or describe their expertise. Even if you think that you have to sound ingratiating or flattering about people's skills and contributions, it is worth remembering that most people like to be respected and given respect for their views.

◆ Produce more support for your ideas. This can be done by using the technique previously described as upward appeal. In this case, you would introduce the following kind of statement: "The managing director and I had a long discussion about this very point and he agrees with me . . ."

SUMMARY

It is worth remembering that every presentation is essentially a performance and how you perform is central to the success or failure of what you are trying to communicate.

Chapter 5

◆

Selling Yourself

There is a well-known, though unwritten, rule in sales that to be effective you need to sell *yourself* before you can successfully sell your product. *Selling is communicating.* Because most of the communication process is nonverbal, the type of body language you adopt is likely to make all the difference between success and failure.

The interaction that takes place between buyer and seller has often been the subject of caricature. This is because buyers have money

Subservience personified

and power, while sellers need to sell to justify their role. While selling is a service, the salesperson will fail to achieve success if perceived as servile. Dickens's Uriah Heep portrayed himself as "the 'umblest person going," but his servility was essentially manipulative, and buyers don't like being manipulated.

THE GROUND RULES

The five examples of power that we discussed in Chapter 3—*position*, *coercion*, *reward*, *expertise*, and *charisma*—also apply in the sales situation, though with a different emphasis.

Remember who you are (position power)

Sellers generally have less power than buyers for the simple reason that buyers can say "Yes," "No," or even, "Convince me." Over the years, business practice has come to recognize the status differentials between buyers and sellers, with the result that more significant titles have been invented to take account of the relative lack of *position power* of sales personnel. Gone are the days when you would carry the small white card saying Sales Representative. Today, you are more likely to have the title of Regional Sales Director, X & Y Consultant, Account Director, or even Assistant Publisher.

There is always a danger that if you don't recognize the relative lack of power in your position as a seller, you will offend, put off, or irritate the client. Taking account of this displays your recognition of the other party's need to be respected for showing interest in you and your product. Therefore, don't keep the buyer waiting and don't allow your body language to convey messages of urgency, aggression, arrogance, or insincerity.

This means that you should maintain a respectable distance from the client (between two and four feet), and alter your standing posture so as not to give the impression of towering over your client. Door-to-door sales personnel are actually told to step back when someone opens the door. This indicates that they are nonthreatening and have no intention of invading the client's space.

Having established your position in the transaction, how you speak to the client is all-important. Much of what you convey is by tone and speed of voice, indicating sincerity, trust, and reliability.

Make the client feel comfortable (reward power)

Making the client feel comfortable is an essential part of establishing a good rapport. Some sales personnel find that making notes during the course of a meeting helps to reinforce the status of the buyer by making her feel more important. Others bring gifts and free samples with them—think of all the pens and pads that pharmaceutical reps leave behind in doctors' offices.

> **Note:** If you give something to another person, however small, there is an obligation on their part to want to agree with you or buy your product. We knew a manager once who would always offer a colleague a mint before he asked for a favor; once they took the mint, they found it difficult to say No.

It goes without saying that the interaction between buyer and seller should be rewarding to the buyer—that is, if you want to see her again. Thus, the mannerisms adopted by the seller should always be polite and respectful, though not overtly ingratiating.

Selling is a sophisticated business and without self-assurance and a convincing manner, no amount of information, gifts, or promises will work for you. A relaxed manner and a sense of humor are often all that are needed to win the day.

A relaxed manner will win the day.

If the seller makes the buyer feel that she is a valued customer, it is a subtle way of rewarding her continuing interest. Also, the product itself is a type of reward in that, with the right deal, it fulfills the buyer's requirements.

Persuasion, not coercion (coercive power)

If rewarding the buyer is part of the psychology of successful selling, then it stands to reason that coercion is not. You seek to *persuade*, not bully or manipulate. The buyer, on the other hand, might use coercive power to try to manipulate you, and this is when you need all your wits about you.

The coercive buyer can get away with being aggressive toward you, being rude when it suits her, and testing your patience just to see how far you can be pushed. Often, such people will use postures and gestures that reinforce their coercive power. This is because clients have *purchasing power*, and it is your job to serve them. You may be seething under the surface, but if you keep your cool, you will come out the winner.

By taking note of the buyer's body language, you will soon learn how to interpret it. For example:

◆ *Superiority* can be deduced from a posture in which the hands are clasped around the back of the head with the elbows pointing outward.

◆ *Critical evaluation* tends to be indicated by the chin leaning on an upward-pointing index finger.

◆ *Impatience* is shown by fingers drumming on a hard surface, combined with sideward glances and snorts of disagreement.

◆ *Disagreement* or even disbelief is shown by shaking the head slightly from side to side.

◆ *Understanding* is shown by a slow nodding of the head while nodding more quickly indicates agreement.

◆ *Confidence* and having made up one's mind is indicated by steepling.

Successful salespeople want long-term relationships with clients. Some enjoy getting new business (hunters), while others like to revisit clients regularly (gatherers).

Be cautious about being the expert (expert power)
Selling undoubtedly relies upon expertise, although care needs to be taken before playing the expert. The seller may know considerably more about the product than the buyer, but it is often better to play this down and to let the buyer feel confident and knowledgeable about the subject.

Sometimes the buyer will convey a sense of giving way to the seller's expertise, but this may be as much to test the substance of the seller's knowledge and experience as to learn about the product.

Noting the tone of voice can make all the difference here. If, for example, the buyer says, "I see, tell me more," you can take this to mean any of the following:

◆ *I am interested; go on.*

◆ *I'll humor her for the moment, but I'm not convinced.*

◆ *I do not believe you for one minute.*

The real meaning behind the buyer's questions are in the tone of voice, not the words.

Your response to ambiguity of this kind needs to be positive and should seek to affirm what you have already been saying. Open body language is all-important here. You want to come across as confident and assertive; therefore,

1. maintain eye contact.

2. smile (but don't grimace).

3. keep an upright, open-body stance.

4. remember that palms down expresses certainty.

Whatever you do, have faith in yourself. There is nothing worse than looking down, as this suggests resignation or defeat. Also, fidgeting can be seen as shiftiness and the client may lose trust in you.

If the buyer does not have the expertise and knowledge about the product or service and clearly indicates that you are the expert, then here is your chance to adopt the consultant style of selling where you solve their problems and difficulties as part of the sales process. The consultant style is shown through assertive gestures and postures and more confidence in the tone of voice.

Be sincere; look the part (charismatic power)

Successful salespeople tend to be outgoing and often extroverted individuals. Some are genuinely charismatic and exude enthusiasm and charm and have little difficulty in holding the interest of their clients. Others work hard on their presentation skills to make up for a lack of spontaneity. In both cases, what makes them successful is their sincerity, and they achieve this by matching their body language with their words.

Remember, charisma is in the mind of the beholder or, in this case, the mind of the buyer. What's more, charisma on its own is not necessarily a touchstone to sales success, so do not *try* to be charismatic; just develop your expert and reward power and the charisma will develop itself.

BODY LANGUAGE IN TELEPHONE SELLING

If you watch colleagues talking on the phone, some of them will feel as if they are in face-to-face contact with the person on the other end of the line. Body posture and gestures tend to be reflected in the tone of voice, so adopting the wrong posture, even on the phone, can give the wrong impression to the listener.

The point is that most telephone communication is restricted to paralinguistic cues; what you think and how you feel are conveyed through *voice intonation*. And it is how you *sound* at the other end that determines the type of reaction. It has been suggested that the word "phony" actually derives from the sensation, first described during the early days of the telephone, of mistrusting the disembodied voice.

Body posture certainly conveys information about the caller. It has been observed that people tend to lower their height slightly when talking to a superior on the phone.

Obviously, the salesperson should sound confident, friendly, and enthusiastic, but this can be quite difficult in the context of a cold call, where the individual you are calling doesn't know you. One way around this situation is to psych yourself up by deliberately adopting a positive frame of mind and an assertive body posture before you start the call. Not only will this make you sound more self-assured, but it will also make you feel more confident. For example:

◆ Try standing with your head up as you speak, rather than sitting slumped at a desk.

◆ Smile when you talk; it comes across in your voice.

◆ Reflect the other person's speed and tone of voice; most of us do this automatically as it is a way of making us feel similar to, or on the same wavelength as the client. Needless to say, if the client is aggressive, abrupt, or has a voice impediment, this could be self-defeating.

◆ Tune in to the client's way of thinking. As we saw in Chapter 2, people tend to "think" in three main ways: sight, sound, and feeling. By recognizing the particular kind of language— images—being used, the salesperson can subtly alter her approach to the client, thus increasing the chances of getting on the same wavelength.

THE CLIENT'S TERRITORY

When you enter the client's territory you are almost certainly at a disadvantage, and as such you will probably touch your cuffs or your watch with one hand as a mild *defense mechanism*. As a rule of thumb, it is advisable to arrive early and to avoid sitting down on the chairs and sofas provided in the reception area. This is because being seated lowers your position, whereby shaking hands and making eye contact becomes more difficult. Also, sitting down can give the impression of lacking respect for the client's authority.

The buyer's office

Going onto a client's territory is one thing, but entering the inner sanctum of the office is another. Since business is about buying and selling, and since we know that the seller needs to respect the buyer's status in order to give the right impression, body language now counts for a great deal.

◆ Standing too upright or too close to the client comes across as too pushy or aggressive, so lower your height slightly.

◆ Standing less than two feet from your client is too intimate and nine feet is too impersonal; the correct distance is between two and four feet. (In Arab cultures closer proximity is acceptable, so consider cultural differences.)

◆ Be aware of posture congruence and interactional synchronizing—adopt similar body postures and gestures but do not deliberately copy as it comes across as contrived. Probably the best method is to use *crossover mirroring*, where the seller imitates the buyer's hand gestures with head movements.

◆ Never adopt a more relaxed posture than the buyer; remember your position power.

A mild defense mechanism

◆ The desk is intimate territory so get permission before you place your documents on it and be careful when leaning over it.

◆ Use active listening gestures, such as the head cock, or grunts and nods of agreement.

◆ Maintain eye contact with the buyer to be seen as more honest, persuasive, informed, and credible.

◆ Be aware of hand gestures. Remember that palms up indicate honesty or uncertainty, while palms down convey certainty and assuredness.

◆ If the buyer has adopted the steepling gesture it may mean they have come to a decision. It is important for the seller to mentally note what gestures and comments preceded steepling, as this indicates possible success or failure in the transaction.

SUMMARY

To deliberately use body language as an aid to selling is to miss the point. You are not acting, you are *understanding* and *utilizing* your own natural attributes to your best advantage.

Chapter 6

The Truth
Detectives

UNCOVERING DECEPTION

Those who investigate the honesty of others need to be able to spot the telltale signs of deception without making it obvious that they are doing so. To some extent this relies on common sense and intuition, although training is needed to develop and improve the skills. Part of such training involves the recognition of body language clues—the nonverbal indicators of concealment, falsification, and lying.

Paradoxically, people involved in deception usually try to avoid lying by initially attempting to conceal the truth. For example, they may

◆ fail to answer the question asked.

◆ pretend not to understand it.

◆ remain silent.

◆ feign emotion, such as anger.

◆ pretend they are feeling ill.

If they can't get away with concealing what they are doing, they may then begin to falsify the situation by

◆ inventing a scenario.

◆ telling a tall story.

◆ telling a lie.

To conceal or avoid telling direct lies people will often water down their statements. Richard Nixon's famous counter to the allegation that he authorized the Watergate break-in—"The president would not do such a thing"—is a classic example of this. By depersonalizing the act—taking the "I" out of the equation—he absolved himself of responsibility for it.

For those whose job it is to elicit the truth from individuals suspected of deception, the type of questions asked and the nature of the answers given is all-important. People generally try to water down lies so they sound less blatant.

Stress—the body language of deception

The body language of deception has its own particular signature— stress. This is manifested in mannered behavior that seems out of place, or uncharacteristic of the person. As early as 1905 Sigmund Freud wrote, "He that has eyes to see and ears to hear may convince himself that no mortal can keep a secret. If his lips are silent, he chatters with his fingertips. Betrayal oozes out of every pore."

Stress can indicate deception through

◆ making odd facial expressions.

◆ feigning yawns.

◆ rubbing hands together.

◆ picking fingernails.

◆ stretching.

◆ avoiding eye contact.

◆ pausing for longer than usual, or becoming silent.

◆ exhibiting glazed expressions.

◆ repeatedly clearing the throat.

◆ making speech errors.

◆ alternating the pitch of the voice.

◆ grinding teeth or biting lips.

◆ nose touching.

In some cases, individuals under suspicion decrease their normal expressive hand and arm movements, using them instead to touch the nose, mouth, and brow. Picking at clothing can also be seen as characteristic of guilty behavior.

The anxiety associated with deceiving others can have the following effects.

◆ Shortness of breath

◆ Difficulty swallowing

◆ Dry mouth

◆ Flushing or blanching of the face

◆ Sweating and palpitations

In extreme circumstances the liar's body may even appear frozen, with arms and legs tightly folded in a defensive posture.

Postscript on nose touching

It is understood that when people tell lies, or even hear other people lying, they tend to touch their nose. There seem to be two explanations for this gesture. First, by touching the nose the hand covers the mouth where the lies are coming from—children often cover their mouths when telling lies. Second, when people tell lies it causes stress, and stress causes the skin to get slightly hotter—the basis of the lie detector machine. When the skin gets hotter, the nose, which is a sensitive organ, may itch or expand slightly, so the individual touches the itching nose.

The whole truth

Uncovering deception applies to job hiring and evaluation interviewing as well as to security screening. People are just as likely to try to pull the wool over the interviewer's eyes. In a survey of 1,500 companies it was found that 71 percent had encountered serious lying on résumés. The most common lies were 31 percent about previous experience, 21 percent about education, 19 percent about previous salary, and 18 percent about secondary qualifications.

So how does the interviewer manage the situation? It has been suggested that subtle rewards and punishments should be used when distinguishing between perceived truths and lies. For example, if the interviewee appears to be speaking honestly,

◆ the response should be friendly and open, such as using the palms-up gesture.

◆ first names should be used.

◆ the interviewer should look directly at and smile at the interviewee.

◆ personal space can be increased between the two of them by leaning or moving back.

On the other hand, if the interviewee appears to be imparting something less than the truth, then the response can be more confrontational. For example, the interviewer can

◆ use gestures such as finger pointing.

◆ look at the individual for slightly longer than usual or look away.

◆ use the subject's surname rather then his first name.

◆ lean forward to decrease personal space.

The aim here is to counter the apparent deception and draw it out into the open.

A word of warning
As a word of warning to the overly zealous—nonverbal communication provides clues to how people think and feel, not evidence. Just because someone appears nervous or behaves uncharacteristically does not prove wrongdoing.

BODY LANGUAGE IN SECURITY AND CONTROL
Those who guard, control, observe, or investigate, such as the police, security personnel, and credit bureaus, have the responsibility of protecting the public. Although they are responsible for helping people, their presence can, under certain circumstances, appear threatening.

For those directly involved in security activities there is, therefore, a need to balance the perception of helping with control, particularly if the public views their services in a positive light. In recent years, for example, armed police have maintained a presence at some major international airports.

It is precisely for this reason that armed officers must be seen to be alert and professional, yet relatively inconspicuous. If they were to act inappropriately—leaning in doorways, chewing gum—

they would undoubtedly alarm the very people they were sent to protect.

It is the ability to spot inappropriate or out-of-place body language in others that enables security personnel to respond quickly to complex situations and to distinguish between those that carry a threat and those that do not. For example, the panic brought on by a mother losing sight of her child in a public place would not be interpreted as threatening, even though the body language of those involved might indicate high levels of anxiety and stress.

During one training course a female airport security officer reported that she had apprehended a woman who was carrying drugs strapped to her body. The woman looked pregnant but, according to the security officer, her suspicions were aroused because the suspect didn't have a "pregnant face." Such sensitivity to detail—the language of the body—has a lot to do with intuition, or having an experienced eye for the unexpected.

Airport security—high stress, low tolerance

Experts have found that more verbal and physical aggression is exhibited at airports, train stations, bus stations, and ports than in most other public places. Airports, in particular, are subject to high levels of such *stress-related behavior*.

Why? According to the experts, it is because travel, and especially air travel, is innately stressful; just getting to the airport can be a nightmare—traffic jams, detours, accidents, panic over missing the plane, things left behind, and so on.

The two most common causes of anxiety are

1. fear of flying. It has been found that people exhibit ten times as many signs of tension (displacement activities) at airports as at

train stations. Only 8 percent of the passengers about to board a train showed these signs, but the figure rose to 80 percent at the check-in counter of a transcontinental flight.

2. loss of personal space. Aggressive body language arises when people are forced to wait in lines, are crowded into restrictive spaces, or feel crammed into airplane seats.

The notion of personal space is also culturally determined. In the United States and western Europe, one's own space is said to be anything under an arm's length; in Mediterranean cultures, it is under elbow length, while in eastern Europe it is about wrist length.

Given that people of all cultures regularly mix at airports it means that levels of tolerance are bound to differ and clashes will occur. When they do, those in the front line at airports who are responsible for managing the public—immigration, customs and excise, police, security, and airline personnel—have to deal with whatever arises while remaining polite, calm, and in control.

Recognizing tension

Being able to recognize tension in others is a first step toward limiting confrontation and alleviating stress. The cabin crew is specially trained to watch for telltale signs of tension, particularly among fidgeting passengers, which can include

◆ repeatedly checking tickets or passports.

◆ rearranging hand luggage.

◆ dropping things.

◆ constantly making "vital last-minute checks."

◆ changing positions in their seats.

- ◆ grimacing.

- ◆ head scratching.

- ◆ earlobe tugging.

- ◆ lighting but not smoking cigarettes.

- ◆ repeatedly breaking matches.

- ◆ rubbing the back of the neck with the palm of the hand.

When tension cannot be displaced in these ways, it begins to flow over in the form of aggression. Sometimes this may be directed at inanimate objects such as airport furniture or through door slamming. At other times it may be targeted at airport staff verbally through argument and confrontation, or nonverbally in the form of aggressive body language.

Staff who find themselves at the center of an incident, for instance, when a disagreement threatens to become physically aggressive, may, quite simply, have been insensitive to the moods and feelings of those they are dealing with. For example, any or all of the following can result in increasing the conflict.

- ◆ Raising one's voice

- ◆ Pointing

- ◆ Rolling one's eyes in frustration

- ◆ Standing too close

It has been noted that some security staff tend to be involved in more incidents than others and it is often their body language, tone of voice, or other mannerisms that make them incident prone; to put it simply, they have inadvertently caused the problem to escalate.

Ambiguous gestures

One of the problems with gestures that people use when they are anxious, angry, frightened, or belligerent is that they can mean different things to those of different ethnic or cultural backgrounds. What may be insulting in one country might not be in another (see page 18–19), and what might be considered a light-hearted gesture to some can have serious implications to others.

In Saudi Arabia touching the lower eyelid with the forefinger indicates stupidity, although in other cultures the same gesture implies secrecy or disbelief. Tapping or twisting the forefinger against the temple are also variants of the stupidity gesture, but since in some cultures these imply that you have a screw loose or that your brain is going around and around, it could be that misinterpretation will result in aggressive counterreaction.

Similarly, the Greek *Moutza*, in which an open hand is thrust toward another person denoting "Get lost," means "Stop there" to police and security officers in Great Britain. Using both hands with the palms held vertically might reduce the risk of misunderstanding.

Another "Get lost!" gesture can cause problems if incorrectly interpreted. This is the chin flick, which occurs when the back of the fingers are swept upward and forward against the underside of the chin. While this gesture means "Get lost" in France and northern Italy, in southern Italy it means "No," or "I do not want any."

Predicting aggression

There are a number of gestures that exemplify aggressive behaviors that can be useful predictors of potential conflict situations.

1. Shake the fist at someone, thus expressing contempt.

2. Execute the hand chop or hand slice, whereby the hand is used like an ax to suggest execution.

3. Prod with the fingertips in the direction of another person's eyes.

4. Point a finger, which is less aggressive than prodding, but nevertheless threatening. For those in security who need to get someone's attention it is better to use the whole hand to point rather than the forefinger.

5. Stare or eyeball, as boxers do before a fight, which is designed to intimidate or control a situation.

6. Crowd or invade someone's personal space, which is also about control. Standing in close proximity has long been known as a means of exerting pressure (raising stress levels).

Obviously, exerting pressure in this way can be interpreted as coercion and such techniques need to be used with sensitivity and care. Fortunately, most threats of aggression do not result in physical violence as most people ultimately prefer to avoid injury.

For those involved in security and crowd management it is important to note the precursors to actual violence, the nonverbal signals that body language betrays. One of the giveaways in this respect is what is known as *adrenalizing*, in which part of the body's fight or flight response comes from adrenaline being pumped around the system in preparation for action. In such cases, breathing tends to speed up and deepen, sweating occurs, the mouth begins to feel dry, and the individual may lick his lips and start swallowing. His face turns pale and he starts to shiver—symptoms that have been described as "the cold sweat of fear."

At the same time that the nervous system is gearing up for action, body posture begins to alter. Squaring up is the body's response to signals of danger. Here, the eyes narrow, the mouth widens, the shoulders are raised, and the neck and head are thrust forward. The arms tend to be slightly bent and the fists begin to clench. As the trunk pushes outward, the abdomen contracts and the knees bend to give more spring in defense as well as attack. The whole process makes the body appear more compact and in readiness for combat.

Avoiding confrontation

There are certain basic rules that should be followed in order to resolve the confrontational situation to everyone's satisfaction.

- ◆ *Be assertive*, not confrontational. Problems are rarely solved through confrontation or argument.

- ◆ *Remain calm* and try to make sure that your own body language is neither defensive nor threatening. You need to be seen to be in control.

- ◆ *Keep at arm's length*. This allows you to step aside if the person might lunge at you. Never attempt to touch or grab someone who is angry as this will only encourage retaliation. You can always tell if you are getting too close, as people will usually step back, lean back, or fold their arms in a defensive posture.

- ◆ *Don't talk down to*, or use gestures that could be interpreted as an implication that the customer is stupid—something more likely to inflame than calm the situation. People are not stupid. They may be difficult, confused, slow, muddled, or even disabled in some way, and you especially have to give the benefit of the doubt to someone with sight or hearing limitations.

◆ *Don't shout* or raise your voice at the customer. Shouting is an aggressive way of communicating and is likely to annoy not only the person you are dealing with, but also those in the immediate vicinity.

◆ *Avoid pointing* at people. If you want their attention, or you wish to direct them in a certain way, use your whole hand. Try not to point directly at individuals. Even pointing with the thumb, nodding, and tossing your head in a certain direction are regarded as surly gestures and are likely to cause irritation.

◆ *Don't beckon with the forefinger only* as this is often perceived as demeaning or sarcastic. It is better to roll the fingers toward you with the palms up, although in Italy, Spain, South America, Africa, and Asia the same gesture is used but with the palms face down. When dealing with children or large groups it is acceptable to use the whole arm to beckon, but this should be done slowly so as to avoid the impression of rushing people. You may have noticed that tour guides and military personnel raise the whole arm above their heads while rotating the forefingers, meaning "Come around me."

◆ *Maintain eye contact* with the customer or client to show that you are interested and concerned. Looking down or looking away may be construed as disinterest and cause annoyance.

◆ *Avoid dissent*; that is, try not to shake your head or wag your finger. If you need to say "No" it is better to use the whole hands, palms-down gesture, while at the same time maintaining friendly eye contact.

◆ *Maintain an upright posture* when sitting, as this appears attentive, professional, and lacking in tension. Slouching, draping legs over chairs, or putting feet on desks appears disrespectful, and leaning back with your hands clasped behind your head and elbows sticking out looks superior.

◆ *Avoid picking at clothing*. The effect of this gesture is to indicate that you are not in agreement with someone and that you can't be bothered to argue.

◆ *Show understanding* when the person you are dealing with is getting flustered. Simple gestures, such as patting the palms in a gentle, downward motion, combined with comments such as "I understand your feelings, so let's talk about it," can make a difficult situation less confrontational. The age-old tradition of offering tea or coffee at such times might also not be a bad idea.

SUMMARY
An understanding of nonverbal communication can help identify stress and deception and also help to foresee conflict and reduce confrontation.

Chapter 7

Are You Listening?

JOB INTERVIEWING, EVALUATION, AND COUNSELING

The interview

Every good manager knows that the aim of an interview—whether for hiring, evaluation, or counseling—is to encourage the interviewee to do most of the talking. This means that the person conducting the interview should be an active listener as well as a questioner.

As a rule of thumb, interviewers should aim to ensure that the interviewee does the talking for about 75 percent of the time in a job interview and evaluation situation, and up to 90 percent of the time in counseling. Listening, of course, means more than simply hearing the words. Being receptive to the cues that interviewees give through their body language is just as important.

First impressions

In the case of job interviewing, the first impression the interviewee and interviewer have of each other often irrationally determines the outcome of the hiring process. The interviewer must be aware of such prejudices and the role that body language has on creating these first impressions.

The interviewee is usually nervous and will tend to talk freely, openly, and honestly only when she begins to feel a rapport with the interviewer. The interviewer has to be careful not to prejudge the interviewee on the basis of these initial signals; the word *prejudice*, after all, means to prejudge. Research has shown that when we first meet others we automatically make judgments about them, such as personality, intelligence, temperament, working abilities, suitability as a friend or lover, and so on.

Sometimes it is intuition that informs us, in the sense that we subconsciously draw conclusions from *body language cues*. These make us feel secure in our understanding of the person without actually knowing why. Interviewers, therefore, need to take stock not only of their inevitable prejudices—particularly relating to social class, gender, ethnic background, dress, and appearance—but also of the speculative manner in which initial judgments are formed. Here are some simple rules for neutralizing first impression bias.

1. Be prepared to recognize your own prejudices and make allowances for them.

2. Remember that assumptions are not facts and do not constitute evidence.

3. Treat each interviewee the same and try to ask the same questions, so that an objective comparison can be made between candidates.

Getting comfortable
In all three types of interviews, getting the interviewee to relax at the very beginning is important, as people tend to be more open and honest if they feel at ease. So don't begin the process by sitting behind a desk as this tends to create a physical, and therefore a psychological, barrier. It is often better to sit on low chairs around a coffee table or opposite each other at one end of the table, as this creates a more relaxed atmosphere.

"There is something about this candidate I do not trust."

Breaking the ice

The interviewer's initial questions should be very informal in order to encourage a natural dialogue. You might want to approach a counseling session obliquely in order to reduce any possible tension by asking simply and with a smile, "Have you done this before? Don't worry; it's easy," followed by (a palms up) "How can I help?"

However, don't

◆ start off with an accusatory tone of voice or remark.

◆ lean too far forward—it's aggressive.

◆ point—also aggressive.

◆ sit back with arms and legs crossed—it shows defensiveness.

◆ lean back, hands behind head—it shows superiority.

If you appear aggressive, too formal, or superior, you will delay getting to know each other and give the other person less of a chance to participate effectively. You may even witness her *physical retreat* as she folds her arms and crosses her legs defensively.

Active listening

The interviewer as an active listener should sound interested, smiling, nodding, and maintaining a reasonable degree of eye contact to encourage rapport. She should be watching as well as listening, in order to take note of the other person's body language:

◆ Cocking the head shows that you are actively listening.

◆ Nodding the head slowly suggests that you are listening and want the other person to continue.

◆ A more rapid nod gives the impression that you agree with what you are hearing.

These are nonverbal forms of encouragement and are essential to maintaining the subject's flow of conversation. It also suggests that you understand and that you are taking in what is being said. But be careful. While this type of nonverbal agreement may be appropriate to evaluation and counseling situations, in job interviewing you may be giving your own views away with the result that the interviewee responds according to what she thinks you want to hear.

On the other hand, some managers are so intent upon conveying a neutral or professional approach that they conduct interviews— especially for hiring—as if they are playing poker, the expressionless poker face. So, remember that if you don't smile, nod, or provide other paralinguistic forms of encouragement, your neutral body language may well be self-defeating; your interviewee will stop talking.

Taking notes

In job interviewing and evaluating you should be making brief notes. If a table is there you may be tempted to use it to rest your notepad on; however, this will cause you to look down and, thereby, break eye contact. Quite often, the interviewee will interpret this as time to stop talking, so it is better to use a clipboard in order to maintain eye contact.

Relaxed posture, easy rapport

If neither of you are relaxed, you will not get the best out of the interview situation, so watch out for defensive postures, such as

◆ leaning back.

◆ arms folded, ankles crossed.

◆ a tense smile.

Research indicates that unrelaxed postures not only reflect but create tension. Most of us know that smiling makes us feel better, as does a relaxed posture. In fact, it helps us to open up mentally, so awareness of your own body language can actually make you think and feel differently.

There are various ways to encourage relaxation. Having a cup of tea or coffee not only sets an informal tone, but also stops the interviewee from adopting a closed or defensive posture, and thus a defensive frame of mind.

When counseling an employee, look for the postures that can tell you whether something is wrong, such as

◆ drooping shoulders.

◆ failure to maintain eye contact.

◆ a sullen expression.

◆ looking down.

These all suggest a negative frame of mind. In such cases, the individual is literally feeling down. Similarly,

◆ self-protective wrapping, in which the arms are folded in front, may suggest withdrawal, or a need to feel safe.

◆ fidgeting and changing position suggests anxiety and nervous tension.

"I'm okay—nothing wrong with me."

Dealing with sensitive issues in an evaluation

If you need to give people *constructive feedback*, which is a better phrase than *criticism*, being assertive but nonthreatening in such situations is important. There are four basic stages that you need to follow if you want to appear sensitive rather than threatening: *introduce*, *expand*, *expect*, and *close*.

1. *Introduce*: As a manager you should attempt to introduce the issue in a neutral and nonthreatening way, being careful to use the kinds of words and phrases that the other person uses.

Above all, avoid any approach or use of posture and gestures that might cause the other person to retreat, feel defensive, or to react in a hostile manner. In a case, for instance, where an employee's punctuality is in question, a blunt approach will just create defensiveness, whereas an assertive though nonaccusatory approach will be more likely to get the right results.

2. *Expand*: Having described the situation in a neutral or non-threatening way, you now wish to expand on why the issue you are raising is important. This requires empathy on your part—being able to put yourself in the other person's shoes.

Here, your tone not only reflects that you understand the employee's point of view, but that you are also showing concern for the team.

3. *Expect*: Having introduced and expanded on the issue, you should now say what you expect from the employee so there are no misunderstandings in the future.

4. *Close*: Now comes the part where you want to finalize the discussion. You may wish to point out the negative consequences if things don't improve; however, you may want to conclude on a positive, optimistic note.

You can vary the procedure according to the employee's response. For example, if she is apologetic after the situation has been introduced, or gives an impression that things will improve, then there may be no need to proceed with the other stages.

Throughout, you need to listen to the tone of voice and speed of delivery and to take note of both verbal and nonverbal signals before responding accordingly. This makes you an active listener.

Maintaining rapport

In all three interview situations the interviewer's job is not to *interrogate* the interviewee, but to *facilitate* the communication process.

Having established a rapport, how do you then maintain it? In a sense, getting along with someone involves synchronizing one's responses to the other. We all do it, often without realizing it. Some experts have gone so far as to argue that rapport involves matching and mirroring body language and tonality.

This doesn't mean exactly copying another person's behavior. You can use *crossover mirroring*—the matching of an arm movement with a small hand movement, or a shift in posture with a corresponding movement of the head. This gives the impression that you are in sympathy with the other person.

In a similar way, changes in facial expression, tone of voice, and use of the hands can make it equally clear that you are disengaging from the conversation. This effectively unlocks you from a "duet" and has been called disengaging from the dance since it breaks the pattern of matching and mirroring.

Rapport can also be maintained by being sensitive to the words the other person uses. We explained in Chapter 2 how different people might think in different ways: *visual*, *auditory*, and *kinesthetic*. By using the same kind of language as the other person, the interviewer soon finds that she is, so to speak, on the same wavelength.

Touching

One of the more contentious issues to do with maintaining rapport concerns actual physical contact or touching. In the United States and Great Britain, touching work colleagues, especially subordinates, is far less common than on the European mainland, and in some cases, it is frowned upon. This is too bad because the simple gesture of touching someone to show support, encouragement, agreement, or gratitude tends to be received with warmth, thereby reinforcing rapport. Sometimes, it is very helpful to touch someone, such as after a difficult evaluation or counseling session, when reaching out a hand to lightly touch an employee's arm, shoulder, or back can be construed as a gesture of support.

Among people of the same sex, a pat on the back—preferably the shoulder blades—by a more senior manager is also likely to be seen as a form of reward. Indeed, it can be a highly significant gesture, as the expression, "I was touched when she thanked me," indicates.

It has also been observed that people are more likely to touch others when giving information or advice, which suggests that touching is a type of *reinforcement* of what is being said. Similarly, we touch each other when asking a favor rather than granting one, or when listening to other people's worries rather than having them listen to ours. It's as if we're saying, "We are friends, so can you help me out with . . . ?" or "I understand. Tell me about it."

Fact or fiction?
We have talked about uncovering deception in security situations where the concern is deliberate concealment and falsification. In evaluations and counseling, you more often find people in denial or being "economical with the truth," that is, covering up for their weaknesses and failures.

In job interviews the one thing that the interviewer needs to know for sure is whether the interviewee is telling the truth about her qualifications, experience, and skills. Asking for documentary evidence and references is a partial way of checking someone's honesty, but face-to-face interviews can help you distinguish fact from fiction.

The astute interviewer can usually pick up hints of self-deception or denial from observing the interviewee's body language. Sometimes, the body is telling a different story from what the words convey. Take the case of what we call "uncomfortable truths."

> *You come across an issue during the course of discussion that you follow up in order to gain clarity. Instead of the straightforward answer that you expect, the interviewee becomes silent. You press further and you get an exaggerated response—a shifting of position, crossed arms, attempts to avert your gaze. When you suggest that the issue is perhaps not quite as clear as was first assumed, the interviewee vehemently denies that the situation occurred, or argues that it cannot be construed in the way that you are describing it. What do you do?*

If you press much harder the chances are that you will lose rapport altogether. The point here is whether or not you have found out what you were looking for. In job interviewing and evaluating you would undoubtedly have touched upon a weakness or a concealment of some kind.

In the counseling situation you *encourage* rather than press the individual to open up and, in the process, you may come across a problem that is masked by the reaction. Even if there is an uncomfortable truth involved here, what you don't do is put pressure on the person to talk. Sensitivity to what is going on behind the scenes is all-important.

Taking the strain

When people are under too much pressure it tends to show in their moods, body language, and ability to cope with everyday tasks. Popularly referred to as *stress*, this much-abused term has come to mean almost anything in our working lives that has to do with being under pressure.

Actually, stress is a natural state of readiness for action, rather like the stress you put on a car's suspension under normal load. *Strain*, on the other hand, describes what happens when a person's natural resources cannot adequately cope with the demands being made upon her.

For those who have limited control over their working lives, stress is a normal phenomenon. But when it becomes too much and things start to go wrong, more often than not it is because someone in a superior position has failed to identify and deal with the situation.

There are many ways in which strain manifests itself. Usually this is when people who normally cope reasonably well with pressure start to exhibit the body language signs of irritability—anxiety, aggression, and tension—or, at the opposite end of the scale—lethargy, apathy, and depression.

Very often, people who are under strain will convey through their body language that something is wrong. For example, they may

◆ become hypersensitive to mild criticism, or even to helpful advice.

◆ display tense postures.

◆ show irritation, such as shrugging the shoulders or casting their eyes to the ceiling.

On the other hand, if the problems are closer to the surface they may

◆ appear restless.

◆ tremble.

◆ exhibit nervous laughter or incoherent speech.

You may even notice pronounced signs of distress, such as

◆ sweating.

◆ eye dilation.

◆ increased swallowing due to dryness of the mouth.

Being able to read and understand pressure signals is essentially a matter of experience. During interviews it is always worth noting signs of discomfort as these may indicate that something is wrong. As we mentioned previously, false yawns, artificial smiles, hand rubbing, picking at clothing, averting one's eyes, and fidgeting, are all common indicators of stressful behavior.

BODY LANGUAGE OF STRAIN

To the experienced eye, the body language of strain is not difficult to detect. The slight stoop of the depressed person, the recurring backache of the overloaded employee, the hangdog look of the defeated coworker, the distracted glances of the anxious supervisor are all indicative of problems that are failing to be identified or alleviated.

The sympathetic touch

It is important to realize that working with people's feelings is a skill that some perform more naturally than others. Learning such skills often requires you to get in touch with feelings that are beneath the surface and often come out in posture, gesture, and tone of voice.

A common mistake made in these situations is to confuse advice-giving with counseling. You can be a good listener, you can be empathetic and encouraging, and you can come up with solutions to surface problems, but you may not actually recognize the underlying causes or be able to deal with their unexpected consequences.

If, as a manager, you find that an interview—particularly over disciplinary issues—is turning into a counseling session, you will need to change your approach. This may involve referral to a counselor. If you do proceed, you will probably find that you are dealing with one or more of the three main causes of emotional turmoil:

1. Guilt

2. Loss

3. Failure

One of these may be relatively simple to unravel but, in combination, they can pose a considerable problem in terms of management. Sometimes getting to the source of the problem is masked by anger on the one hand and fear on the other, and only sensitive probing will enable you to gain the confidence of the person in question to talk about how she feels.

It is essential to note the body language of overexpressive, anxious, and unfulfilled behavior:

◆ The tautness of anger

◆ The hangdog look of unhappiness

◆ The hunched, burdened look

◆ The listless, apathetic, depressed coworker

◆ The shrunken posture of failure

◆ The darting eyes of guilt

◆ The wracked expression of loss

◆ The hollow-eyed look of fear

It is equally essential to note the verbal cues that people give you, language that expresses physical or psychosomatic ailments. These can sometimes be a guide to stress at work:

◆ Backache very often relates to lack of support.

◆ Laryngitis relates to speechlessness.

◆ Stomach trouble indicates not being able to tolerate something.

◆ Tension headaches can be caused by pressure.

◆ Breathlessness comes from a fear of performing badly.

◆ Blurred vision leads to panic or a loss of perspective.

In fact, many physical conditions that we might never think of in terms of emotions have directly similar parallels.

Once you have gained the insight into these issues and the skills to effectively deal with them, they will become natural to you and you will find that people increasingly relax in your company.

SUMMARY

The understanding and awareness of body language gives the manager the clues and insights essential if she is to move from mere manager to the modern role of coach and facilitator.

Body language provides the manager with a whole new world of insight and understanding. It is like putting on glasses for the first time when you become nearsighted—and for those of us who do wear glasses we can truly *hear* better with our glasses on.

Index